A FAMILY 'S JOURNEYS THROUGH PRAYER

True Stories of the Power of God

M. Diane Cressman

A FAMILY 'S JOURNEYS THROUGH PRAYER

Copyright © 2010 by M. Diane Cressman

Cover art by M. Diane Cressman.

Portrait art by Lissette Martinez.

ISBN 978-0-9844087-9-5

This book is dedicated to all those who choose to walk with God and to those who through trials and sufferings are trying to find their way to God.

Especially to my husband John, who's always been that silent strength in our family. The man who taught me to laugh and to try new things in life. The man with an adventurous soul and a man young at heart.

To my children whose taught me all things are possible if you believe as a child, not wavering but believe what God says. To watch them grow into great Christians and raise their children to love God and to pray. For the countless times we've laughed, cried, talked and prayed together and even fussed together. They now have children of their own and God is about to show them poetic justice. Their children will someday be teenagers.

To my 14 grandkids whose smiles and laughter makes life worth living. For being a part of Gods plan to remind me how fast our children grow and what a treasure they are. They remind me to believe in miracles and not to give up.

In Memory Of

In Memory of my parents, Alice Elizabeth Hill Murray and Clifford F. Murray. The world was a better place because they were here and taught us not to give up. It was in the hard times of their lives, they did not give up. They taught us to work hard for what we wanted and pray for the rest.

Acknowledgments

First, I would like to thank my family for the support I've received and the encouragement to write this book, especially my oldest son, John who set everything in motion and encouraged me to finish the book. He has always been in my corner to listen and encourage me with his famous words to me "you can do it."

A big thanks to my grandkids whose innocence and faith reminds me daily how blessed I am. Saying I love you comes easy with forgiveness. We can learn so much from them.

To our oldest and dearest friends Sam and Cindy Wilcox whose Christian walk has always been inspiring and a joy in our lives and to this day, we call them family. They have lived the example of what a real Christian is.

To Diane and Neil Brantley who took us under their wing 42 years ago and helped us grow spiritually by their example, true friends, real friends and solid Christians. Their friendship has been a gift from God.

To Pastor John Strictland of the Virginia Creek Ministries that encouraged me to finish this book. For giving those inspirational down to earth sermons that inspires us to keep living our lives for Christ. He is a man after God's own heart.

To Karen and Ronnie Tyndall who became our new Christian friends down at Virginia Creek Campground, whose example of faith has been inspiring to all they meet.

To Marylin and Jack Adams for their help in proof reading and editing the book. Thanks for all the help in correcting my southern slang so the book could be read by all. Their Christian walk has made them the giving and serving people that they are.

Thank you all, for being the best part of my life.

Foreword

When trials come, Christians look for answers. They want to know why is this happening. Why would God allow me to go through this? How long is this going to last? Where is God? What are trials and why do we need them? In these series of books they will take you along on the journey of a family of eight, their trials and difficulties. It takes you through their lives, how they reacted and their response to God in their lives. You will share in their anger, tears, miracles, hopes and enduring love for one another. Reading this book may answer some of your own questions you have put to God. It is a book of hope and encouragement. It shows God's enduring mercy and love for a family. The same love he has for each one of us.

Table of Contents

Introduction 1

Chapter 1 - The Tribulation Years 13

Chapter 2 - Johnny's Miracle: Trial by Fire 19

Chapter 3 - David, Daniel Boone and the Fort 29

Chapter 4 - Poisoned by the Kiss of Death 37

Chapter 5 - A Pair Of Shoes and 25 Cents 47

Chapter 6 - God, John and Momma 53

Chapter 7 - Johnny, Moses and Snakes 57

Chapter 8 - Melody's Angel 61

Chapter 9 - Out of the Tribulation 65

Chapter 10 - God And The Impossible 69

Chapter 11 - A Retreat from the World 75

Introduction

This book is about the trials and tribulations of an ordinary family of eight whose trust and faith in God was tried and tested as they went through some very difficult times in their lives in a very short period of time.

I hope that as you read this book you will be encouraged and inspired to be able to look at my family and look at your own life to see what God and His incredible love for us has done and is doing for you. If God can work things out for us then He can answer your prayers. Look at the best and never give up and realize that God will work things out in His own time.

A FAMILY 'S JOURNEYS THROUGH PRAYER

In this book, I will take you through my family's journey. It is their stories of God's power working in their lives. I chose to write this book to share with others the love God has for each human being. I am like you, no one special, except to God. I am a normal person like you. There is no PHD after my name. I am a grandmother of 14 grandkids, a mother of 6, a wife of 42 years, one of 7 children, but most of all a Christian. I found out that I mattered to God.

Our Christian journey is like a roller coaster ride. It has many ups and downs. When we're going up, we feel exhilarated, refreshed, enjoying the ride that someone else is controlling and what an awesome feeling it is. Then the ride approaches the top and begins to slow down and you are looking straight down into what appears to be certain death. You just kind of freeze as this ride races down. There is nothing you can do about it, but hang on for dear life. Your heart races, you lose your breath, you tightly grip anything you can. Your feet and legs tighten up on anything they are touching and you scream out. As you glance back at the operator of the ride, you wonder if he knows you are going to die.

Introduction

You wish you could just stop the ride and get off. Desperately you want to walk back down where there is safety.

Our lives are much like that ride. When things are going good and we feel great, it is easier to believe God is in control. But when things go bad, we look back at the operator and ask "Where is God"? Is He in control?" As Christians we wish we could get off because we don't know how long the trial will last or how it will end.

I have been a Christian for over 42 years and during those years I have kept journals of my prayers and talks to God, and things we as a family went through. This book shares a lot of my family's trials, and growth as a Christian family, the good, the bad and the ugly. Just like David a man after God's own heart, you will see a family that made mistakes, got angry at God, argued with God, tried to justify their actions to God, and asked the age old questions," Why ? Why me? Why is this happening to us?"

A FAMILY 'S JOURNEYS THROUGH PRAYER

Have you ever gone on a journey? Sometimes we set out on a journey, only for that journey to be halted by things going wrong. Maybe you took the wrong turn or your car runs out of gas. There is a possibility that you will have several breakdowns that get in the way of you reaching the end of your journey or even an accident. A lot of the times, most people will get frustrated and quit, turn around to go home. They do not want anymore inconveniences to happen or feel it was not meant to be. Sometimes we don't think the journey is worth all the hassles.

As a Christian we are on a journey to make it into the Kingdom of God and Satan will fight you, putting every emotional and spiritual obstacle in your way. Through the different series of these books you will come to see how this family found the answers to all the why questions in the midst of their journey. You will ride along on their rollercoaster ride, the ups and downs. Although it is 42 years later, we are still getting the answers to why we had to go through what we did. You will find that is so true. Years down the road you can say," if it had not been for going through that heart wrenching trial, I could not have made it to this point in my life."

When I was young, I could not understand why David was so loved by God. Why was he known as the man after God's own heart? David lied; he committed adultery and committed murder. David had so many family issues, murder, rape and family turning away from God. So why was David so special? As I have grown and matured as a Christian I have found the answers to those questions. David was as human as they come, but when David made a mistake and was aware of his sin, he deeply repented. David didn't just pay lip service, he repented from his heart. He chose to live and rely on God.

The Psalms are full of David's prayers, pleads, forgiveness and thankfulness. The Bible is full of stories of the trials God's people have gone through and as you read the stories you come to understand why they went through it and you get to see the outcome of humans making wrong choices. You get to look into their lives and see how some turned to God and how others walked away from God. The question is how will your story play out? Will you turn and draw closer to God or will you take the easy way out and give up?

As we grow as Christians our lives should become an example for others. We should find that we are praying more and building Godly character. Forgiving others should come more easily as we mature as Christians. In these series of books it is just that, a family of eight going through trials, growing spiritually, the tears, pains, miracles, blessings, anger and God's unconditional love for us even when we did not deserve it. We even experience God's correction in our lives. God says He corrects those He loves. In answering our prayers God takes so much in consideration, these are only a few.

First - In answering this prayer, is it the best for us at this time in our life?

Second - In answering this prayer will it bring us closer to God, or lead us away from God?

Introduction

Third- In answering this prayer will it be an example to others, to build faith, inspire, encourage or lift up?

Fourth- In answering this prayer is God helping us out temporarily until we are stronger spiritually for the next trial or until we learn what He is trying to show us. Sometimes we have to learn to crawl before we learn to walk and then learn to run.

Very seldom does God answer prayers like we think He should. God considers all things and all people involved. We are so often like children, we want it now, and we don't want to wait. We question what is wrong with God; He should give it to me when I want it. Sometimes God's answer is just no, not now, you're not ready. So like the humans we are, we take matters in our own hands, and God has to come along and straighten out the mess we have made. Our impatience is sometimes our worst enemy.

In the movie "Lord of the Rings", Frodo tells Gandalf "I wish this never happened." Gandalf replies, "it's what we do with what we   have   been   given". That is so true in our Christian journey. God watches us to see what we do with what He's given us. So often we make mistakes that hurt not just ourselves, but others. You cannot change what has been done, but you have the power to learn from your mistakes and change what lies ahead.

Martin Luther King wrote," the true measure of a man is not where he stands in times of comfort and convenience, but where he stands in times of challenge and controversy."

How true is that statement in our Christian walk with God? It is easy to love, praise and give thanks to God when everything in your life is going well. But how long would it take you to get angry, to lose faith, to blame God? What if all of a sudden tragedy struck and continues on for years? What would it take to break you, for you to lose faith? How long would it take you to give up on God? The book of Job is a great example of faith in God when everything goes wrong. Job did not only lose all he had, his wife wanted him to curse God.

Introduction

Satan is counting on you to give up, to lose the battle, to curse God. Jesus is counting on you to win, to endure to the end. Jesus has never called you to lose, you are somebody. You are special; you have been called to be a child of The Most High Living God. "Being confident in this very thing, that he who hath begun a good work in you will perform it until the day of Jesus Christ." Philippians 1: 6. I often tell my grandchildren, God's Holy Spirit is like the force in the movie Stars Wars , the force is stronger than evil. We as Christians need to use the force (Gods Holy Spirit) against Satan (the dark side).In the end, good will always prevail. We have to keep focus on God.

As we all live in this 21st century, a year of uncertainty, the economy is worse than it has ever been, job losses, homes losses and we as Christians will be tested to our limits. It seems every radical group or animal has more rights than a Christian. Satan is attacking this nation and Christians as he has never done before. God is counting on you to win the battle, to enter unto his gates with praise and thanksgiving. Don't ever give up. If you give up you may not see the loved ones you have lost. Imagine the reunion, what is that worth? God knows, he made the ultimate sacrifice. He gave his only son, so that we could live and be forgiven. That's love. Imagine the reunion God had with Christ. Can you even comprehend the reunion you will someday have with God and Jesus Christ and your loved ones?

Don't ever give up, no matter how hopeless life seems, don't you dare give up? Just like a mother, she will never give up on her children nor will God give up on you.

In my Bible I have this quote written. It reminds me to never give up. I have read and reread this quote countless times when I have felt discouraged and hopeless and fell to my knees to pray. It is called the serenity prayer. So often we read only a part of it.

"God grant me the courage to change the things I can change,

The serenity to accept those I cannot change and the wisdom to know the difference" Here is the rest of it. "But God, grant me the courage not to give up on what I think is right even though I think it is hopeless."

You will face many of those times in your life. It is up to you. God will not force us to choose what is right. We have to want to choose God's way. It is the only way you will win over Satan. He will try to destroy you as he did Job. He will take your very life if God allowed him. We do not know what God will require out of us. But we can have confidence in knowing all that we lose, God will give back. That is what this book is about, waiting on God, trusting God, believing in His promises that He will take care of us and supply our needs. It is about Psalms 37, waiting patiently on God for the desires of our heart. Someday we will see all the ones we loved that died, suffer and the many innocents that were killed. See, Satan cannot see that far ahead, because he does not comprehend the greatest gift of all, which is God's love and forgiveness.

The journey of your Christian walk, your rollercoaster ride is just the beginning. How you reach your destination is another matter. This family of eight will share their journey with you in the chapters ahead and books to come.

Chapter 1 - The Tribulation Years

Some years ago I think it was the latter part of the seventies, because Tammy was three years old. We had begun going through what I like to call our tribulation years, because those trying years lasted three and a half years.

It started when John my husband, lost his teaching job in N.C. for religious reasons. Without going into a lot of detail, I will just say that the county wanted him and all teachers to follow the state rule of only taking two personal days a year. At that time we were keeping the holy days listed in the Old Testament and saw that Jesus and the disciples kept them even in the New Testament so we needed 4-5 days a year. In good conscience, he felt we could not disobey God. It was a witness because he had to explain his beliefs to the whole board of education. Although we got a civil rights lawyer and took it to court, we lost on the grounds they said he needed one more course to get certified. What we failed to prove was that the superintendant would not allow him to take the course unless he signed a paper stating he would not take more than two days off for the religious holy days. We took off 4-5 days a year for three years without a problem. Well, we could not do that. John had gotten substitutes and made the lesson plans up ahead of time so that everything would run smoothly while he was gone. The school continued to use his substitute teachers for other teachers when they were out.

I guess we were just shocked at the result since another teacher went through the same thing and won his case. He had been reinstated and received back pay. So why didn't God hear our prayers? Why didn't he help us? We prayed and fasted about it. What happened? Was the other family better Christians? Why did God not come to our rescue instead of allowing us three and a half years of pain, hurt, and doubt?

After our years of service, where was God? Why did he allow this? We gave a tithe and we gave offerings to help the widows and orphans. We never missed church and we were raising our children to love and trust God, so why?

So much happened in those years. God had His plan and Satan was waiting in the shadows, ready to destroy our family. We felt we were headed around a sharp bend in the road. We didn't know whether we would pull out of it in time.

Our children in that period of time were injured, our daughter almost died. We couldn't get food stamps and they threatened to foreclose on our house. We lived in constant fear not knowing if our lights would be shut off. It was a very stressful time. That was the same time a recession had hit the south. Like today, few jobs could be found. They said John was over qualified to do basic manual labor jobs, now that's sad. Because he had $1000 dollars in his retirement we did not qualify for any unemployment or food stamps. If you ever have the need to be humble and humiliated, try to apply for food stamps. This was a good man who served two years in Vietnam. A man who loved his country and teaching. I have often wondered how a man can lose a job in America for religious beliefs. But it happens. I have to admit I was not a happy camper. God and I went at it a lot, God always won those fights.

We had hit rock bottom and felt deserted by God and friends. When you are going through hard times you will find out who your real friends are. So many of our Christian friends would say, "repent, you must have done something wrong!" Don't you just love friends like that? It sounds like the friends of Job, doesn't it? We received so much support from a widow lady in church, a single girl, Cindy and a single guy named Carl. They were always encouraging and up lifting. The least likely ones in church to get invited out but understood real Christianity.

Where was God through this? Was He out playing golf or what? Why had God allowed this to happen?

Chapter 1 - The Tribulation Years

Why did He allow my children to suffer? Why had our prayers gone unanswered? We loved God, we taught our children to love and trust God. We tried to live our lives as an example. What kind of example were we now?

I think as Christians there will be many countless times that we will cry out the very words that Christ cried out on the cross "My God, My God why have you forsaken me"

Chapter 2 - Johnny's Miracle: Trial by Fire

It was in the fall. We were out raking the leaves and twigs in piles to be burned. Melody, our fourth child was over a month old, so it had to be early November. The children were gathering leaves and sticks on a pile to burn. We had been raking and burning leaves most of the day so we had a big pile of ashes. Although the fire was out, the leaves were still very hot and smothering.

We had just got through telling Johnny not to throw anymore leaves on the fire. He had a twig and bent over to put it on the smoldering leaves and ashes. Johnny lost his balance and fell hands first into the ashes up to his elbows. I will never forget that scream. Johnny started screaming and running. He screamed, "God! God! Help me! Help me!" I ran after Johnny and put his hands and arms under the cold water of the well. We quickly wrapped his hands in a wet towel. The skin was hanging off his hands. The ashes were so hot that it caused the skin to melt off his arm and hands.

John called the neighbor to stay with the kids so we could get Johnny to the emergency room. Johnny was screaming and crying, "it burns, it burns, O God help me!" As I held Johnny, my heart was breaking.

I was trying not to cry while praying so hard for God to take away his pain and save his hands.

As we went into the hospital, Johnny had quit crying. He looked at me and said," It will be all right momma". The doctor examined Johnny's arms and hands. They cleaned his hands and arms cutting the dead hanging skin and put some salve on it. I remember the doctor saying it was vitamin E. The doctor then looked at us in a way that a doctor does when he is about to give you bad news.

Chapter 2 - Johnny's Miracle: Trial by Fire

"Mrs. Cressman your son has severe second and third degree burns. We don't know how much damage has been done to the nerves in his hands or if he'll ever have use of his one hand again. He will need several skin grafts and therapy. We will have to take the extra skin from his hip". "Time will tell, it is a slow process, it is one of the worst burns I've ever seen. I can tell you, he will probably have no feeling in his right hand.

John and I sat there speechless in other turmoil. Out of the quiet, still room, Johnny was the first to speak," God will heal me". So many things were racing through my mind. One overwhelming thought was that finding a job and providing our needs was insignificant to healing our son who was in pain. I began to see it takes a lot more patience and faith to trust God for healing.

Then the anger, why? Why did God let this happen to Johnny? No child deserves to lose the use of his hands and the disfigurement. What else did God want from us?

John had no job, we barely had food, and we were living day to day.

The doctor bandaged up Johnny's hands and arms and we went home. We were to take Johnny back on Friday for a follow up visit to discuss the skin grafting and therapy. We called the church and asked for prayers for Johnny. It was amazing that Johnny had no pain so we assumed it was from the nerve damage in his hands. Every day we prayed and asked for God's healing. Johnny said to me, "Momma, I'm like Shadrack, Meshach and Abed-nego, except they were protected in the fire and did not get burned. I did, but God's going to heal me, because it doesn't hurt anymore. "I prayed to God and He is going to heal me."

As I hugged Johnny I prayed, "Great God, do not destroy his faith. This little boy believes more than I do."I smiled at Johnny and said God does heal, sometimes we just have to wait patiently. "Yep," said Johnny," and you got to have faith, right Momma? "Right, Johnny". But as I said those words my heart was filled with fear. Then I remembered, love cast out fear and I had so much love for Johnny. That night we all prayed for Johnny and waited for the next day, Friday, when the doctors would remove the bandages.

Friday came and as we walked to the Doctors office Johnny was skipping and smiling. The doctor looked at me as he removed the bandages. "Don't expect too much? He will need plastic surgery, skin grafting and therapy. We will just have to wait to see how much damage has been done", he said. As the bandages came off, I do not know who was more shocked, the doctor or me. Johnny's hands looked almost completely healed. We each sat there with our mouth wide open, except for Johnny. Johnny said, "see I told you God would heal me." The doctor picked up the vitamin E cream and said, "this really works".

The doctor asked Johnny if he could feel anything in his hands and Johnny said "yes, ever since we came to the hospital and God healed my hands", When was that Johnny, I asked? "When we first came to the hospital and my hands stopped hurting"

That was one of many miracles God performed in our family. Johnny will be 41 years old and to this day doctors says he has 3 plastic surgery marks on his hands. It has continued to be a witness to others and Johnny still tells people, "God healed me". Would you believe Johnny works with his hands as a computer technician, magician and a hypnotherapist? So for someone who was told he may never use his hands again, Johnny makes his living with his hands.

When I look back on this time in our lives, my question was why God? I found the answer. God never left. A child's unwavering faith, which is what he wants from us. I learned that is exactly what God wants from us, unconditional love, trust and faith. I know that when everything in your life seems to go wrong that is a sign for us to get right with God. God is looking to build his character in us and we are to become the image of God.

I have written in my Bible a saying "the true measure of a man is not where he stands in times of comfort and convenience, but where he stands in times of challenge and controversy". Martin Luther King. So is it with our Christian walk with God.

It is easy to go to church, serve and go on with our lives. We tithe, we are being blessed, our children are healthy, our bills are paid, and our refrigerator is full. But what does it take to continue to trust God, when we lose everything and we're put to the test? What was it that Job said to his wife, "shall we receive good at the hand of God, and shall we not receive evil?" Job's wife was bitter and wanted him to curse God. She had lost her children, possessions and position. Job had open sores on his body, everything was gone except their life.

It's not until we are tested that we find out just how much we need to grow spiritually.

I have seen Christians; good people fall apart, lose faith, and walk away from God when tragedy strikes. When they lose a loved one, a job or home. We become bitter, hurt and blame God for our circumstances. There are a lot of trials we bring upon ourselves and our families. Adultery can break up a marriage and cause a divorce which separates and destroys families especially the children. The misuse of money and credit cards brings money problems. Gossip divides families, friends and sows discord. It steals another person's character. God does not force us to do the right thing. He wants us to choose to make the right decision based on His law.

I can honestly look you in the eyes and tell you, there is nothing we can go through or experience that God is not by our side. We have someone who knows the weakness of man, we have God's son, Jesus Christ in our corner.

This world as beautiful as it is is not what God wants for us. God's hands are off although He still intervenes on our behalf. God will never force us to choose good over evil. God does not make us take drugs or drink and drive. He doesn't force us to look at porn or gamble? God does not make you listen to slander or gossip. God has given us free will and as human beings we mess our lives up.

Chapter 2 - Johnny's Miracle: Trial by Fire

There are consequences for making wrong choices. David is a good example. We can repent and change with the grace of God.

I have raised six children and have 14 grandchildren as I write this book. The stories I share with you is my walk with God through the pain and suffering of a wife, a grandmother, a mother, a sister, a friend, but most of all as a Christian. I am not always proud of how I handled things and the trials in my life. When I look back on that time with Johnny and his burned hands, I realized, that Johnny didn't cry out for me, his mother, when he was in pain. He cried out for God. It was Johnny's faith, the faith of a child, his prayer that healed him.

Luke 18:17 "Verily I say unto you, whosoever shall not receive the Kingdom of God like a little child, shall in no way enter it." A child is so innocent. When you tell them something, they believe it, they don't doubt .I hope I can give you hope and encouragement that our experience can strengthen you in your trials and your walk with God Knowing that He walks beside you every step of the way. God calls winners. He has never called a loser. You can make it. If God didn't believe in you, He never would have called you.

Chapter 3 - David, Daniel Boone and the Fort

It was not long after Johnny burnt his hands that his brother David was tested. During this time, John still did not have regular job. He did whatever grass cutting, lawn care and other odd jobs he could get just to keep the bills paid. He used his VA to go to a community college to learn auto body repair, which would pay off later in life. I learned to cook a mean potato. We lived off of a lot of potatoes in three and a half years. There were a lot of potatoes, rice, oatmeal, grits and day old bread from the thrift stores. Amazingly through this time I don't remember the children ever complaining about being hungry or asking for more.

I had gotten a job selling Tupperware; it was a blessing at the time. Although I would only bring home $20-$50 every two weeks, sometimes less, it helped out toward the bills and gas to go to church. Once in a while we would buy meat. I remember buying a whole chicken for $.59 or $.89 and that chicken made a pot of chicken pastry. Down south, that is fine eating. We thought we were living high on the hog if we had chicken pastry and biscuit.

It is amazing what we take for granted until we don't have it. When John was teaching I could go out and buy bags of groceries. I was lucky now to buy one bag with the bare necessities, soap, shampoo, toilet paper, oil and flour. As long as I had flour, I could make biscuits.

I was off at a Tupperware party and John had the kids at a church social where the men were playing softball. There was a park that had a castle; Johnny and David were on the castle pretending to be Daniel Boone. They thought it was a great fort. It was at least 15 foot high and David being only four and a half years old fell from the castle and broke his clavicle bone (shoulder). John took him to the emergency room where they x-rayed it and put a clavicle splint on it.

When I got home I saw the splint on David and that he was crying pretty hard. You could tell he was in a lot of pain. We were concerned that something was still wrong. We took David back to the ER and found the first doctor put the wrong size splint on him. The doctor put a new one on which helped hold his shoulder up and relieved a lot of the pain up. We then made an appointment with a specialist for that Monday, the next day. I thought to myself, what else God, we're barely over Johnny's hand, now this, how much more can we take?

Doctor Dorman looked at the x-rays and took his own x-rays and confirmed it was broke. We were looking at 8 to 12 weeks for it to heal and then physical therapy. He said to bring him back Friday to follow up and x-ray it again. That night David was crying with pain. John, Johnny, Tammy and I prayed for him. After the kids went to bed David was in his bed still crying, John and I knelt to pray. I must have fallen asleep on my knees because John was in bed. As I removed my hand from David's little hand, he said, "God will heal me momma, don't cry". Out of the mouth of a child came assurance to his momma, he believed.

A peace came over me as tears slid down my cheeks. Where had I heard those words before? I glanced at his brother where just a few months before Johnny had third degree burns, now totally healed. I kissed David and said, "I know David, "and as I walked back to my bed, I prayed and asked God to perform the same miracle He did with Johnny. I asked God to help my little faith.

On Friday we returned to see Dr. Dorman. He asked if David was in any pain and asked the nurse to have new x-rays of his shoulder. I told him that he had not complained about pain since that Monday night (when we all prayed). When the nurse returned with the x-rays the doctor was mad and yelled," I said the x-rays of the Cressman boy ". The nurse said these are David's x-rays.

The doctor took David back to x-ray it himself. When he came back in he was shaking his head saying," it's impossible. The x-rays don't lie."I was worried at his tone and puzzled look. He came over to me. "Mrs. Cressman, I want you to look at the x-rays from the hospital and the x-rays we took of David's shoulder when you brought him in on Monday. They look the same." "Yes, I see them. What is the problem?" I asked. "Mrs. Cressman these are the two x-rays we just took. I don't understand this, it's impossible, but the x-ray shows the bone is completely healed. Mrs. Cressman, there is no way that bone can heal in five days, no way possible." David spoke up, "God healed me, I told you momma. God healed me". I wanted to fall on my knees in that doctor's office.

I wanted to cry out to thank God again for His awesome miracle. The doctor knelt down on his knees to talk to David. Dr. Dorman looked at the three sets of x-rays. "You're right son, God did heal you, and this is a miracle. As a doctor I have seen the unexpected done, and this is a miracle."

Once again God heard the prayers of a child and his family. He was teaching me through all of our trials that He was still there. He was providing our needs. Where there is doubt you won't find faith. David unlike us, had no doubt, and that faith healed him. Little did we know that David would be tested with his own child one day. God would revisit David and heal his daughter and save her and her mom from death.

I've come to see as I get closer to the end of my life, that life is only a journey. A journey that takes us to our final destination, the Kingdom of God. But on that journey we will run into detours, trials, which take us off our main course. Satan is a clever, sneaky and a very patient opponent, like a lion waiting for its prey. He waits for us to become overwhelmed. He waits for us to get discouraged, hurt, troubled, run down, and even lonely. Then he makes sin look good or makes us doubt God. Isn't that what he did with Eve?

Chapter 3 - David, Daniel Boone and the Fort

He convinced her to doubt what God told her. She got Adam to doubt God. Adam blamed his weakness on Eve instead of accepting responsibility for his mistakes. That is one thing even Christians have a hard time with. We don't want to accept responsibility for our mistakes. It is easy to put all the blame on others so we can justify our actions.

Our journey, our walk with God can be exciting, awesome with so much to learn and see along the way. It is like taking a walk and sitting by a beautiful waterfall. We are unaware that just around the bend; a hungry grizzly bear could be enjoying that same waterfall. Satan doesn't want you to finish that journey. He's like that grizzly bear. He will pick up your scent if he's on the attack and hunt you down like a wounded animal. Satan will set out with every human nature trick, known to man, to destroy you. He will wait until we are angry at God and then give us thoughts to blame God. Always keep your eyes focused on the kingdom of God. Stay the course.

Take the journey. You may have detours along the way; God will see you through the job, through sickness and the trials. Don't give up. If a four and a half year old little boy didn't give up, why would you? When you can get down on your knees and pray for your enemies and pray not my will God, but your will be done in my life, then you'll be near the end of your journey. Make the most out of your journey. Look to God to direct you. After all, He gave you a roadmap. It is called the Bible. It will lead you to your final destination.

Chapter 4 - Poisoned by the Kiss of Death

Tammy Diane was our beautiful three and a half year old daughter. I use to tell her that I prayed she would have green eyes long golden brown hair and she does. Tammy was the apple of her daddy's eye and I would dress her up like a princess. She was a chatter box and kept her two older brothers in line, she adored her little sister Melody who was only seven months old at the time. Tammy, like her daughters Paige and Jade could walk in a room and it would come alive with laughter.

It had been a long day. We'd just finished supper. John was in the garage working on a car. He was painting a car for a man and he would always have to spray poison in the garage to kill any insects that could stick to the wet paint. I had just finished giving the kids a bath. It was one of those hot summer nights so Tammy ran outside, in her underwear, to kiss her daddy goodnight and came back in the house.

I notice that she looked pale and was starting to have labored breathing and then began to wheeze. I yelled for John to come in. We couldn't figure out what had happened. It happened so quickly. We were praying and crying out to God. We had no idea what had happened in a matter of five minutes, she was fine when she ran outside. Within minutes, we saw no improvement and actually saw she was starting to lose consciousness so we called for an ambulance. Tammy was semi conscious by this time and when I say it happened so quickly it was a matter of minutes.

John picked her up and started to run up the dirt road. I ran after him and slapped him. I could tell he was in shock. That was his precious daughter he held lifeless in his arms. I said "Go back to the house, call Francis to stay with the kids. I will meet the ambulance at the end of the road" John was in shock. I think he would have run to the hospital carrying Tammy, so I had to slap him to try to snap him out of his state of shock. The ambulance met us at the end of the dirt road. I rode in the ambulance while John got Francis to watch the kids and he drove to the hospital.

The ambulance attendants asked what happened. They asked if she ate anything or could have gotten bit by anything. I told them, I did not know of anything that could have happened .Tammy was now making gargling sounds and choking on her on fluids. The one attendant said," we're losing her..."All I know is that time seemed to go on forever, yet like slow motion. I just kept praying," take me God, not my baby; don't take her this way, where John would blame himself for the rest of his life"."Don't take our baby, our sunshine." Tammy could walk in a room and it would just light up.

We arrived at the hospital, it seem to have taken forever to get there. The ER doctors asked the same questions, they pumped her stomach, nothing, and then

A FAMILY 'S JOURNEYS THROUGH PRAYER

Tammy lapsed into a coma. John arrived at the hospital by this time. The doctor came out and said he thought when she had gone out to kiss her daddy goodnight, because of the warm bath and weather, her body had absorbed the poison through her pores and went directly into her system. Who would have ever thought that could have happened. If I had known that John had just sprayed more poison, I would have never allowed her out. They gave no hope of her coming out of the coma and if she did she would probably have brain damage.

Tammy was put into a room; her once bubbly little body lay motionless. She was in an oxygen tent hooked up to IV's and tubes. Nurses would come in and out checking on her. John and I prayed as if our very souls were crying out. I told John to go home that I was staying and would start fasting until Tammy came out of the coma. I told him it wasn't his fault and if God could heal Johnny and David He could heal Tammy. I think it was in that hospital room that I made my peace with God. Although God had healed our sons and we were barely getting by, I was mad at God. I wanted my life back, I wanted money to buy groceries, I wanted the bills paid, I didn't want to worry any more, and I wanted my children to be well and healthy.

I realized everything that was precious to me lay in that hospital bed; it was my children, my husband. All of a sudden the house, job, nothing mattered as long as we were together as a family. I needed God to give me strength to handle whatever happened .I stayed by Tammy's bed talking to her, telling her how special she was. "Tammy, come back to us, do you hear me?" "Come back to momma, Tammy! Come back, we need you". I was in the third day of fast, John went to church with the kids .He had song leading and they asked for prayers for Tammy, exactly at 2:10 pm. It was at that time I saw Tammy sit up and she was jumping up and down in the oxygen tent. A nurse rushed in and tried to give her a shot. I yelled at her and told her no. The doctor came in and checked Tammy out, they unhooked all the stuff. The doctor looked at me and said" don't get your hopes up, she will probably have some brain damage". I said, "no, God healed this child", they looked at me with pity, thinking I was in denial. I was not in denial. I was in faith and thankfulness.

I had witnessed another miracle God does a job right, he finishes his work, I knew Tammy was healed. The doctor had to give Tammy a shot to counter act what the one the nurse had given Tammy. Tammy said," Momma, I want to go home, God healed me, let's go home". "We will as soon as daddy gets here honey."I said.

When John got to the hospital and saw Tammy he could hardly keep his composure. He couldn't believe this was the same little girl he had just seen hours earlier. Tammy was fine, no brain damage, although at times her brothers to this day swears she does! That's brothers for you. We were so thankful to be taking our beautiful daughter home.

I would like to share with you my thoughts. I wish I could say that I was this strong Christian, and that my faith didn't waver, but that would be a lie, and would defeat the purpose of this book. As I rode in that ambulance I felt like my life was ending. I was crying, screaming inside, "No God! No God! Don't take my baby! Take me! Take me, not my baby." Many of you reading this have already experience that loss, to you I say the only thing I can say," as surely as there is a God who sits on a throne you will see that child or loved one again". Their spirit is with God awaiting the reunion". Do not give up. Do not let your pain and grief keep you from seeing them again. Live your life in the fullness of God, with love and forgiveness in your heart .Ask God to give you the strength to get through it, one day at a time.

And for those who are sitting by a bedside, praying your heart out, begging and crying, pleading, ask God to help you accept His decision. We don't have to like God's decision, but we need to accept it and pray for understanding.   That will be your hardest prayer. Because, I knew I would never get through this without his help. Let's be honest. We don't think anyone can love our child more than us, well God does. I've always felt our children are on loan to us from God. He's the creator, the real father of us all.

A FAMILY 'S JOURNEYS THROUGH PRAYER

A lot of so call Christians would say why cry or plead with God, just accept His will. I guess they never read the Psalms where David pleads and cries out to God, Ps. 22:1-2 "How long will you forsake me". David was very emotional when it came to God. He loved God. He was a man after God's own heart. God promises us an eternity with the people we love if we live our life for God. It does not matter what trials comes your way. He will see you through it. Remember, " all things work for good for those who love God", yes, all things, the pain, hurts, disappointment, loss, even unanswered prayers. Do not give up. We are to build godly character. You will find that in Philippians 4:8, " Finally brethren, whatever things are true, whatever things are honest, whatever thing are just, whatever thing are pure, whatever things are lovely, whatever things are of good report; think on these things: if there be any virtue, if there be any praise, think on these things."

I might just add here about another miracle. You may wonder how a family with so little income, no

44

medical coverage and no welfare or other government subsidies made it with those doctor and hospital bills. When John lost his job, he bought a $22 a month accident policy, which we still maintain until this day. It covered all the bills, even Tammy's. That was difficult because originally the insurance company said it was poisoning and not an accidental injury. We told them we would not intentionally poison our daughter and it was not a sickness so it had to be an accidental poisoning. They finally agreed and paid it. Thank God we kept that policy up, because when he lost his job he lost the insurance benefits. But God did what doctors could not do. He picked up when they gave up hope, all because of a child's faith.

Chapter 5 - A Pair Of Shoes and 25 Cents

During what I call the tribulation years, I got a job selling Tupperware. It was a blessing at the time. John still couldn't find any work. He had been a teacher and worked as a mechanic. John had served a little over four years in the marines. He had spent a little over two of those years in Vietnam. This was a blow to him. It would be for any man, not being able to provide for his family. John did provide, but on his knees. Although John never showed it, I knew he was worried. He believed God would provide for us. He picked up odd jobs cutting grass and worked on people's cars.

Our average income was between twenty to fifty dollars a week sometimes less other times more. The little I made at Tupperware helped out a lot. At that time we had not asked the church for help yet. John often took David with him to cut grass. David would look forward in stopping and getting a $.15 donut with his dad after a long day of working in the sun. To this day, David a grown man still loves working outside with his two children. , His kids look forward in stopping with their dad to get a donut.

We had been praying daily for God to provide our needs. So far they did not repossess the house, we had enough gas to get to church, potatoes and rice was cheap. Thank God our garden was doing great. Johnny, David and Tammy needed shoes. Johnny had holes in his shoes and everyone had out grown their shoes. We knew of a Christian thrift store, so I decided to take the kids down, at least maybe I could get Johnny a pair of shoes.

Chapter 5 - A Pair Of Shoes and 25 Cents

I finally found a pair in pretty good shape but there was no price on it. So I went up the cashier. The lady in front of me had an arm full of clothes and several pair of shoes. Her order came to $2.50 so I figured the shoes would be about $.25. That was all I had. I put the shoes on the counter and the cashier said fifty cents." " Fifty cents," I said, I only have $.25. My husband is not working and my son needs shoes." "Fifty cents" said the lady." "But the woman in front of me just got two bags for $2.50. How can one pair of shoes cost $.50? "Please, I only have twenty five cents and my son needs a pair of shoes." She said she was sorry, but that was the price. I really needed a pair of shoes for my child and I could not even afford a $.50 pair of shoes. I had always given and helped people out. I couldn't understand when we needed help, why couldn't we get it? Satan was working overtime that day.

I took my three children, got in the car and started driving home. As I was driving home I asked God to help me understand why He could not provide my children with shoes? Regardless of what happens in our lives we should never get angry at innocent people. The woman was doing her job. She didn't own the store. I always tell my children not to judge others. God doesn't like ugly, and you can bet if you are ugly to others, God will be the one to deal with you. I still tell my children that today.

Once again, God knew Johnny needed shoes. There is nothing more that can tear at a mother's heart than not being able to provide for her children and to give them what they need. I thought to myself, God, what did these children do? God promised to provide our needs, aren't clothes and shoes needs and necessities? As I rounded a curve I saw a yard sale. I thought maybe I could find something for the children there or least a pair of shoes. The woman smiled and I asked if she had any children's shoes? She said in the bags there is a mixture of children clothes, "I am getting ready to close for the day so you can have all three bags for twenty five cents."

I stood there trying to hold the tears back and I felt so humble before God. He not only provided shoes for all the children but also clothing for all the kids, even a few toys. Tammy got two nice dresses for church and shoes and more clothing. Johnny and David got shoes, shorts, and pants and shirts for church. Johnny loved books and there were books in the bags for all of the kids. God took care of the children's needs. He even went beyond what they actually needed. God knew better than I did what they needed and what would lift their spirits, a few toys and books.

As humans the hardest thing for us to do is to let go and turn everything over to God. That does not mean we are supposed to sit around and do nothing, but when circumstances are out of our control then that is when we need to trust God to do his part. When God provides us with help, when he answers our prayers, they will always be better and more than what we asked Him for. I was so concentrating on Johnny's shoes I didn't stop to think about the other clothes they needed. I thought God would take care of the one with the biggest need. But God, looked at the needs of all the children, he provided their needs. Sometimes God's greatest gift is our unanswered prayers. God knew the needs and the heart of the children and he provided for them. Once again I learned a humbling lesson, trust God with your needs, he will never let you down.

All I know is that God was showing me that He loved us. He would provide for us when no one else would or could. He gave us more than a pair of shoes that day. God was showing us that no matter how hopeless things can appear, He's here with us, waiting for the opportunity to show us, even with a pair of shoes.

Chapter 6 - God, John and Momma

My family, mom, brothers and sisters never really knew how rough

and bad things were for us. They knew that the kids had been sick and hurt but had no idea how bad we were off financially. My father had died while I was pregnant with Tammy so my mom was having a hard time dealing with his death and finances. My family at the time did not understand why we believed what we did, since I had been raised southern Baptist.

It is amazing that as people we often fear what we don't understand. I think that is true to this day. I guess that's why God says knowledge is the beginning of understanding. Do not get me wrong. John and I did not always handle things with wisdom and looking back I can see how we offended my family. As newly zealous Christians we think we can only obey God one way. News flash: self righteousness, God works and calls us all differently. We all have different gifts that God has given us and He calls us all accordingly to His will, His purpose. God does not call us to judge others. He has that job covered by Himself.

John had gotten a car to paint. We were excited because it would have given us the extra money to pay some bills that needed to be paid.

When the phone rang it was Momma. It was unusual for Momma to call because at the time my family wasn't speaking to us. I knew something was up cause Momma sounded like she had been crying. "Momma what's wrong I asked". Momma choked and said she needed some money to make the mortgage payment because she was two months behind, and if we had anything to help her out. Now I can tell you one thing about my Momma, she never asked for anything, so for Momma to call me up and ask I knew it had to be a bad situation.

Momma said when our father died he didn't have but a five thousand dollar life insurance policy and after the funeral she didn't have anything left. Momma always had a rough life she didn't deserve this. "Momma let me talk to John and see what we could do and I'll call you back", I said.

I went outside to talk to John and he was holding the check, the man had paid him for the paint job. It was a check for $150.00, he was smiling. I told him about Momma and what she said. John signed the check and said give it to your mom. There are not many people that would have done that when they needed it so badly for themselves. John was not most people. He was a Christian man. I grew to respect and love him so much more that day. He taught me what real sacrifice and love was. The only thing he said was that God probably provided the car for that purpose, to see if we were willing to help Momma.

See, as Christians it is easy to give and help others out as long as we have extra or plenty. But real Christianity comes in to play when we're tested to give when we ourselves are in need. I think God wanted to help Momma and used us to do it. I know that day was a turning point in our relationship with Momma. When I called Momma back and told her John had a check for $150 for her I could hear the relief in her voice.

In years to come God blessed us financially and we were able to help Momma out each month. It was something we kept between us. I found out years later when Momma died she had told her sister Cindy cause Aunt Cindy brought it up to me when we were visiting her. John and I would send Aunt Cindy a little money now and then. She was a lot like Momma and I think it would have made Momma happy to know we didn't forget Cindy and I think God has always been there to remind us to help others because He helped us so often. We learn by example, always remember someone is watching you.

Chapter 7 - Johnny, Moses and Snakes

When we lived in North Carolina at Myrtle Grove we lived in an area that had swamps and woods all around us. It seems we had wild boar, snapping turtles, and lots of snakes including too many copperhead snakes. I remember sometimes coming home after dark and seeing copperheads snakes lying in our yard. We would hear them slithering away as we walked and saw marks where they slithered across the sandy driveway. We had lots of privacy because we lived in the woods and had just cleared enough land to pull a mobile home up a dirt road and swing it into position. The result was that it was still home to many wild creatures and reptiles.

Anyway, when we got home, John would get out of the car with a flashlight to look for the snakes before we dashed to the house. The worst experience was to have one or two snakes lying on the steps. I remember being scared to death for the children.

One night I was telling Johnny and David the story of Moses and Aaron and how God used Moses' snake to eat the snakes of the pharaoh's priests. Johnny looked up and said "let's pray that God will send good snakes to eat the bad snakes." I laughed to myself and said," Okay, we will pray that God will send the good snakes to eat up the bad snakes". Johnny was telling all about the copperheads. David was about four years old. He just told God to let the snakes be gone. Well, in the next three weeks we saw fewer copperheads. I had not given it much thought .I was just glad that the snakes were gone.

As I walked out to the garden and was shocked to see this huge black snake. I had never seen a black snake in our yard before. As I got closer and looked more careful, I saw it had a copperhead snake in his mouth.

That grossed me out and I ran back to the house. The black snakes stayed on our property for another two weeks. Then I realized that we were not seeing any more copperheads.

UNBELIEVABLE, I know. But yes, did it really happen? Some friends were skeptical about the snake eating story, so I did some research on the internet and what showed up was a photo of a black snake eating a poisonous snake. How about that?

See, sometimes we can laugh at the things our children pray for, but God takes our children very seriously. Johnny and David truly believed God would send a good snake to eat the bad snakes and God did. He taught the woman who laughed at her children's requests that God can do anything. Johnny, David and Tammy believed the stories in the Bible and in their little minds if God can do it for Moses he could do it for them.

Now, do you believe that this really happened? Well, it absolutely happened. This book is a written account of how prayer worked in our lives. Unbelievable, yes, but then we serve an amazing God. God showed me, and I believe in an awesome God.

Chapter 8 - Melody's Angel

John still didn't have work. The recession down south was taking its toll on our family. There were times John had to ask the church for assistance to keep the lights on or pay the mortgage. Our mortgage at that time was around $77. I had started selling Tupperware to help out. One day I had to deliver the Tupperware to a lady. I remember I kept praying "please God, please let her pay me in cash, so I could get some milk and gas on the way home. Well, she did not. It was a check for $26.

As I drove home I stopped at the store to get milk for Melody. With all the stress, I had lost my milk and could no longer nurse Melody. I went through the car and my purse to try to find enough money to buy the milk. I figured I could get at least a pint of milk then drive. If I ran out of gas and I could walk the rest of the way home. We lived about five miles from the store down a long stretch of pitch black highway.

I was so angry at God. All I had was twenty five cents. I hit the steering wheel and yelled at God. It was overwhelming and I started to cry. What had Melody done? She was just a baby. She needed milk, and the car needed gas. I sat in the car calling God a liar and crying. I was at my lowest spiritually and physically, I just felt drained. Finally I just felt I could not go on one more day. "You said if we obey, lived our lives for you that we would not hunger or beg for food. You lied God." After I dried my eyes I went into the store and decided to get milk and I would walk home.

When I brought the milk to the counter, the clerk said, "twenty six cents". I swallowed hard and said "I only have twenty five cents. ", "Sorry" said the clerk. I took the milk back. It took all I had not to lose it in the store. As I started to the door, shoulders slumped,

defeated, the clerk yelled," lady you forgot your milk"."
No", I replied, it's not mine"," Lady, all I know is that a
man came in paid for this gallon of milk and $3 worth of
gas. He said it was for you and your baby." What? "Lady,
it's yours, take it or leave it". I took it. Back then three
dollars would almost fill a tank.

God proved He does not and cannot lie. I cried, I
sat in the car and just cried. I asked God for forgiveness
for doubting Him, for the lack of faith for not trusting
him. I sat in the parking lot for over an hour talking to
God, thanking him for the healings of our children and
for the loving kindness He had shown our family, for
always providing our needs. That night God sent an
angel to pay for the milk and gas. There was no one else
in that store. How did the clerk know I had a baby that
needed milk? It wasn't the clerk. I believe it was an angel
sent from God. I believe that it was probably Melody's
guardian angel.

I believe we all have angels watching over us and I
think God allowed Melody's angel to provide for her. In
Matthew 18:10 " Take heed that ye despise not one of

these little ones; for I say unto you that in heaven their angels do always behold the face of my Father, who is in heaven."

The following day, John got a job, a real job, not as good as teaching but it paid the bills. That night was a turning point in my life. I knew we were going to be alright, no matter what, we would make it. "If God was for us, who can be against us?" Sometimes we are our own worst enemy. We let fear get in the way of faith and hope, even love. That was one of the things I had to come to see over and over again. Fear destroys hope. Fear and real faith cannot dwell together. I had to learn God was our only hope. We had to have faith in His promises, even when we didn't understand His reasons behind the trials we went through.

Chapter 9 - Out of the Tribulation

After three and a half years of what I call the tribulation years, no job, children getting hurt, the economy started to change, and John was blessed with a job. Melody was born in 1976. She was just a baby during those three and half years. In 1978 I was pregnant with our fifth child, Carl. We had decided to sell our house and buy a larger home. We had found a miniature plantation with 9 acres of land and a garage for John. We thought it would be the perfect place to raise our children and have a big yard and garden. After such a difficult three and a half years we were ready to start fresh. I was so happy. I thought God had given me my dream home. There were apple trees, grapevines, blueberry bushes and pecan trees.

During this time, John had wanted a teaching position in his home town in Pennsylvania. He had applied at Lehigh County Vocational Technical School and really wanted a job teaching auto mechanics. We were informed he did not get it so we put the money down on this house, we had been approved and our house had sold. I was at home, happy about all the changes in our lives, thanking God for our new home.

The telephone rang. It was someone from the vocational school that noticed on his application that he had auto body experience and they were offering him the job of teaching auto body repair at double the salary he was making now and triple what he was making teaching in NC. Have you ever had a moment where everything flashed in your mind and time stood still. I could see the house of my dreams. We could be happy to stay in North Carolina. Was I being selfish?" Mrs. Cressman I need a decision, someone else wants the position." I heard myself say," Yes, John wants the job". "Good, I will send the contract out. He needs to sign it and send it back." "Thank you," I said. I will give him the message".

As I hung up the phone, I questioned whether or not I had made the right decision. I just gave up the home of my dreams and worst yet, leaving North Carolina. Later John came home and we were sitting down at the table to have supper. I told him the school called and they wanted to know if he still wanted the teaching position. As I looked into his puppy dog eyes I could see and hear his anxious question. "What did you tell them"? The look in his eyes and voice told me I had made the right decision. "I told them that you wanted the job, but it wasn't the auto-mechanic position, it was for the auto body position. You got the job! We have to be in Pa. in five weeks." Are you kidding?", "No, I am not kidding, you got the job." That night was a night of rejoicing in our home. The down side was that we would lose the deposit we put on the house.

After everyone went to bed, I took the picture of the house and folded it up and placed it in my Bible. As tears fell down my cheeks, I was scared, I didn't want to move. I didn't want my children to lose their little southern accent. I didn't want to leave Topsail. There was a part of my heart that was breaking and I didn't know how to stop it. I asked God to help me, to accept his decision, to walk through the doors He had opened for us. I still have the picture in a file cabinet, 33 years later to remind me how quickly God can change the course of our lives.

It would take 13 years before I would get my dream home. Life is a journey. Moving to Pennsylvania is just additional chapters of a family's journey through prayer. Believe me when you have teenagers, you need prayers, miracles and a lot of mercy.

Chapter 10 - God And The Impossible

The last two chapters are skipping ahead to thirteen years later and thirty years later in time but I thought this would be a good note to end this first book of a series of books to come on a family's journey through prayer.

Years ago when the children were mostly teenagers, John and I decided to look for that dream home. It was never about if the house was big and fancy. We wanted a larger home that could accommodate our large family. We needed a lot of bedrooms, because we had six children. John was making more money teaching now, so we could afford a bigger home. The children had adapted to living up North and yes, they lost their southern accents. We all sat down at the table to discuss what we needed. We needed a big kitchen, large living room and hopefully a family room, at least five bedrooms, a garage for John, and of course the kids wanted an in ground pool. We told everybody to start praying about it and see what door God would open.

Well, the search was on. Every time we found a house it seemed like we would have had to change the garage and family room into bed rooms, or the bedrooms were little or it had a little kitchen. It didn't help that we only had a budget of $115,000. I know what you're thinking, but you're forgetting this family had seen God work miracles in their lives. The average home was between $129,000 and $179,000 dollars. We thought we had to settle for what we could find which was very frustrating.

David got really mad because we kept getting outbid on homes. I told the kids, "Let's pray about it because God knows what we need." David had an attitude. "Right mom, we're going to ask God for a big house, big kitchen, lots of bedrooms and a garage for dad, why we don't just ask God for a big in ground pool while we're at it," he said in frustration. "Yes David, we will. God can give us the desires of our hearts, if we trust him. If these houses don't work out it's because they were not the houses for us. God will find that house. Be patient." I said. "But you keep saying that mom and we can't find a house," David said in frustration. David was angry. Everyone was getting disappointed. We had been praying and searching and it was hard to find anything we could afford. "Then we will just have to wait until God finds the right house," I said to David.

A few days later I saw an ad in the paper, I told my daughter Tammy "Let's go look at it, it sounds too good to be true." Tammy was driving by this time. We drove around for over an hour looking for this house. We could not find it, so we decided to go back homes a different way. That's when we saw a sign, "Open House."We turned down the road to find the house we had been praying for. The realtor told us to look around. She said they had put the wrong address in the paper and we were the only ones to come to see the house. It was a bank repo and needed a lot of cosmetic work done to it. I asked the realtor if they would take VA. and she said they would. The kitchen was huge, a nice dining and living room, 3 bedrooms upstairs and a large bathroom. We went downstairs and there was a huge family room with a fireplace. There was a large laundry room and two other rooms that could be bedrooms. Then off the family room was a 13 by 36 foot room that over looked a 46 foot in ground pool with a barbecue pit and patio.

Tammy and I were squeezing each other's hands and trying to hold back our excitement. We went upstairs to ask the scary question, how much? I just knew this house was way out of our budget. The realtor told me the price $122,000, I asked if they would accept an offer of $115,000. She said she thought the bank would approve. I asked her if my husband and kids could come over to see it when my husband was came home from school. The realtor said yes and that she would stay until 6 pm. I called John and told him to come home right after school and we would all ride over to see the house. When everyone saw it they all knew.

Chapter 10 - God And The Impossible

I looked at David and said, "Look out of the dining room window." His eyes nearly popped out as he hauled buggy down the stairs with the other kids and John behind them. When they saw the pool, squeals came out. John looked at me and said, "Are you sure about the price?"I said, " yes and I told the lady we would take it". John looked at me like I was from a different planet and said," Are you sure this is the one"? I do not make decisions like that, so for me to tell the realtor we would take it without talking to John first was unusual to say the least. "What do you think, it has an oversize 2 car garage and three fourths of an acre corner lot" I said. He looked at me and smiled, "this is it". That night the house was bubbling over with how they were going to fix their rooms and when we got the keys, we all went over and everyone jumped in the pool with their clothes on, except me. Later on we realized that God had His own plans for us to move. One of those reasons would be to save Melody's life.

God never does anything half way. Once again he looked at all of our needs and threw in a big bonus, a huge pool. I am sure God heard David mocking Him and God had the last laugh, as well as taught David a lesson. That house entertained many Christian families and rocked 14 grand babies, now how does life get better than that? A house bought for $115,000 now worth $300,000, God is always looking after us in ways we can't see.

John and I have raised our children in this home so it will be hard to sell this big 2800 square foot bi-level home. The kids are all grown and busy with their own lives and children. We are looking to down size and I am sure God will lead us to the right home once again at the right time. We just want to take this time in our lives to enjoy each other and fall in love all over again. To find a smaller home with low maintenance so we're free to go back and forth to Topsail.

Chapter 11 - A Retreat from the World

The reason I decided to add this chapter was because I think it's important for Christians to get away from their every day routine and take the time now and then to renew themselves spiritually. Sometimes we need a place to be alone with God, to renew our relationship with Him. We need a place to take time to reflect on our Christian growth and to get our priorities right. A chance to stop and appreciate the beauty of nature God has given us. Do you want to believe in God and see if God does exist? Get into nature and you will believe, because nature teaches us in a creator.

After raising six children and watching 13 grandchildren at that time, I needed a place that I could go to and renew my spirit. It's too easy to get caught up in family problems and trials. It can take the toll on us spiritually and emotionally. That is true with our jobs, our church our everyday life. Since moving to Pennsylvania it seem our life was like a merry-go-round. We came out of a period of trials just to enter different ones. But you will have to get the next book to find out what happened after leaving North Carolina. It is when the North meets the South. After forty years of trials and raising children John and I needed a place to go and rest.

The first place I thought of was Topsail Island. I had lived on the Island as a teenager and fell in love with the peacefulness and tranquility of the Island. Once you have seen a sunrise over the ocean or a beautiful sunset over the sound you have it forever etched in your mind. Have you ever sat on a beach with calm waves and watch dolphins at play and listen to the seagulls singing their songs. I have, and I can close my eyes and see it all, that is Topsail Island.

Chapter 11 - A Retreat from the World

I have always wanted to go back to Topsail. I wanted to walk the beach and talk to God like I used to. It was at Topsail Island that I devoted my life to God, seeking His will in my life, asking him to direct my path, which at that time I thought it was to become a missionary nurse or join the Peace Corp.

I had been very unhappy as a teenager and the girls at school treated me like an outsider. We had moved from Four Oaks in Johnston County from our farm. It was a difference of night and day moving to Topsail. At that time I felt I had entered the twilight zone. The beach life and kids were totally different from the down to earth farm life I had lived. So many could have spoken up but their silence hurt, sometimes teenagers can be very cruel. In our youth we do and say cruel things not realizing how those things can effect and hurt others. I always had a lot of things to talk over with God as I walked the beach of Topsail.

It was at Topsail where I met my husband, a Marine that just came back from Vietnam, searching for that Christian woman. It was at Topsail, that God sent three dolphins to save me from a shark for reasons only He knows. It was at Topsail Island where John and I were baptized over forty two years ago in Surf City Baptist Church. It was the same church we were married in on Topsail Island, North Carolina. I guess you can tell how much Topsail Island meant to me.

Whenever I would get discouraged, I would go to Beltsville State Park, here in Pennsylvania. At the beach area, overlooking this huge lake surrounded by the Blue Mountains, mountain laurel and blue spruce trees. The mountain laurel is a flowering bush which is a lot like the azaleas in North Carolina. I would go down, sit on a bench, close my eyes and see Topsail in my mind.

I could envision everything except for the smell of the salty breeze blowing across my face and the sound of sea gulls as they soar above the clouds. I wrote a song down there called "Headed to Carolina". I would go down to Beltsville to sit or walk with God. Until we moved to Topsail Island, I missed the farm we were raised on in Johnston.

Chapter 11 - A Retreat from the World

It is strange, as I write this final chapter in this book, that I am sitting overlooking a huge creek (more like a lake) that flows into the intercoastal waterway. I can sit on my porch and smell the salty breeze and see the seagulls and heron, even a pelican. John and I can walk down to the dock and stare out at a beautiful sunset. All I have to do is drive 5 miles and I'm on Topsail Island. Once again, God looked into my heart and gave John and me the desires of our hearts. Just remember this came 32 years after our tribulation years. Hopefully, we will be able to enjoy the sunset years of our live at the campground and Topsail Island.

I had mentioned to John that I wish we could find a little place close to Topsail. His answer was "We can't afford it." The only way we're going to get anything close to the beach will be when you win the lottery" Fine, but if God wants us to get a place at Topsail, you can't stop him," I said. I put a big box in the garage and John wanted to know what it was for. One day, I finally told him that it was for our beach house. He laughed and said good luck with that. Every time I saw something I thought would look good in our beach house, I'd put it in the box. The kids laughed, but I kept putting things in the box.

One day while we were in N.C. visiting family, we checked out some of the seasonal camp grounds. We really didn't like what we saw, the campers were too close, no shade, too loud, just not for us. As we were leaving I saw a sign that said Virginia Creek Camp Ground. Let's go check it out I said to John. We drove to the office and asked the receptionist if we could look around. She said yes and off we went.

Well, it was awesome. There was a dock for fishing, a place to launch kayaks and canoes. The campers were not as close to one another and you could add on a screened in porches. We both fell in love with the place and went up to the office to see if any sites were available close to the water, Mary said no, and that they had people on a waiting list to get sites by the water. I asked her to put our names down on the list also. I said," If God wants us to get one by the water, we will."

Chapter 11 - A Retreat from the World

It wasn't long before we got a call from the campground. They wanted to know if we were still interested in a site by the water. She told us that one was available and no one else on the list had gotten back with her, so she was offering it to us. I talked to John and we decided to take it. I called her back and we had a campsite overlooking the water.

The only problem was that their policy changed and now our camper was too old. I was looking on the computer one day for campers when this web site popped up. It was in New Jersey and I found some real nice campers. I gave them a call, they took some information and they said we qualified and to come down to take a look. John and I drove down to see what they had. We had in mind what we wanted. The one I saw on the web site was nice but just was not what we wanted. We checked out the others and finally walked into our little dream camper, 40 foot long with 3 slides, used only once, it was perfect. When we talked to the man, everything worked out better than we had hoped for.

Once again God provided the right camper at the right price, at the right time. Our son in-law pulled it down for us and set it up. Joel was awesome. When we got back to PA we sold our older camper and smaller camper and trailer. We sold it for just enough to build the deck and screened in porch. It turned out to be awesome.

Virginia Creek Campground has become our refuge, a place to go and relax, kayak, canoe, fish, bike, study and pray. It gives us a chance to reflect and renew ourselves spiritually and physically. One of the greatest gifts that came out of getting the site was the new friends we have made and so many Christian friends. The fish fry Mr. and Mrs. King puts on for everyone are great. I can't imagine anyone passing up a fish fry and Karen's hushpuppies. You will find the best cooks at the campground. I think John drives to the camper just to get some homemade collard greens and southern style vegetables and I would drive for all the yummy deserts.

God knew I needed to come back to Topsail, if for no other reason it was to write this book. John and I realize that we have been so blessed. We have the best of both worlds, the beach at Topsail, Virginia Creek Campground and to be surrounded by the Blue Mountains of Pennsylvania. The Blue Mountains is a sight to behold. It looks like someone is handing you a bouquet of gold and red flowers. The mountains become alive with a rainbow of color with the autumn leaves in September and October.

As I write this book my dear friend Karen found out she had leukemia. It came as a shock to all of us at the campground, because we feel as we are all one big family. That's what God's Holy Spirit does, it binds us together. When one suffers we all suffer. Pastor John Strickland and his wife remind us of just that. Karen and Ronnie will have their mountain to climb, but God will be beside them helping them along the way with outstretched hands. They will have so many Christian friends like Linda, Buddy and the Kings and us. Too many friends to mention. I ask that you remember them in your prayers.

I really hope by reading this book it has inspired you. There are so many miracles waiting to happen in your life. Hey, if God can love me and my family so much, then you've got it made. Just remember that you are a miracle of God. He created you to succeed, to overcome. He called you to be a child of God and if you are a child of God, you will always have God by your side every step of the way.

Don't give up on yourself and those you love, no matter how hopeless things look. God has a plan for you. Satan does not want you to win. He does not want you to overcome. He is the dark side of life. Do as Yoda said, "use the force", use Gods Holy Spirit in your life. Don't be afraid to ask God."You have not, because you ask not" also "what is impossible with man is possible with God" and my favorite, "I can do all things through Christ Jesus who strengthens me" You are called to win the battle, "if God be for us, who can be against us?"

As I close the final chapter of this book, I would like to answer the question "Why?" Why did God allow my family to go through these trials and our children suffered? Well, I am still finding out the answers to those questions. Sometimes when I think I know the answer then God shows me more every day. At that time in our Christian life, we hadn't really been tested. We had to learn what was really important in our lives. You can sit in church every day, tithe, visit the sick and still not make it into the Kingdom of God. It takes having the proper fear of God; it takes real faith, the type of faith that casts out the wrong kind of fear. It takes love, unconditional love. It takes daily repentance and forgiving others.

Sometimes we are unaware that we hold God back from blessing us. It is simply because we do not forgive others like God says we should. We judge others and remind other people how wrong they did us. It takes getting to know God through His word, the very character of God. What does God requires of us? Seek the answer to that question and you will be a very wise person.

Why did all of these things happened, because God was looking to build godly character in us. God loved us, He loved my children, and He knew they had faith. See they walked the walk, and not pay God with lip service. So often we as Christians get caught up with service that we forget to speak to the person not dressed like we think they should be. Maybe they have too many tattoos or they don't have all their teeth. We judge people without even knowing it. We're asked to pray for others but why stop there? Send a card, make a phone call or email. Follow up with those people.

Do you realize that we can offend a newcomer in Christ by our lack of involvement? So many people have walked through the doors of churches just to get hurt and offended by the actions of what someone said or did not say. We look to the deacons, elders or minister as perfect people. News flash: they are as human as we are and they are growing and learning spiritually. Maybe they have too much responsibility on their plate and they need to get their priorities right. I don't know. That is between them and God. You don't have to be an elder or deacon or minister to encourage or help someone. You just need to ask God to give you the wisdom to recognize a need and to act on it. God gives us all gifts and talents, but it's what you do with the gifts and talents

God gives us. Look for opportunities to encourage, help others and to lift others up.

I found out I had so much to learn about being a real Christian. God taught me many lessons of faith. When most of our Christian friends were busy pointing out what we did wrong, like with Job, God sent a widow, a single girl and a single man to encourage us and show us what real Christianity is. It wasn't the deacons or elders, but a widow lady and two singles. I have seen God intervene in our lives, miracle after miracle. I may not have liked or understood God's reasons for it at the time, but I have learned if there had been any other way to have brought me to my knees any quicker with the right results, then God would have found it. I had to learn about real trust and real faith and I can tell you now, those tribulation years brought me to my knees and closer to God than anything else.

Listen to me, people are human, they may let you down, but God will never let you down or leave you. In a world that has gotten so far from God we need to renew our hope and faith in a God who is in control.

Remember in Romans 8:28 "And we know that all things work together for good to them that love God, to them that are called according to his purpose." And didn't God say in Romans 8:31, "if God be for us, who can be against us?" In verse 35 of Romans 8, "What shall separate us from the love of Christ?" The answer is in verse 35-39 of Romans 8. Read it and you will come to understand how important the trials and testing us are to God. God wants to see us build faith and trust in Him, to put on the whole armor of God.

We are in a battle against Satan for our spiritual life. God will do whatever it takes to help us prepare for that battle. The question to you is, are you ready for that battle? Ephesians 6:12-17, will be your secret weapon against Satan, read it and use it. It is your only hope and means to win the battle. In any battle, it is the one who endures to the end that wins. The last man standing. Are you ready to put on the whole armor of God to fight until the end? It is up to you. There is no one that can get you through the battle. It will be you and Christ fighting side by side against Satan. You can do it.

About the Author

M. Diane Cressman was born in Robinson County, NC, one of seven children. She lived in Johnston County, NC. where she was raised on a farm in Four Oaks until her family moved to Topsail Island, N.C. where she lived until she married. She lives now in Pa. but stays in N.C as much as she can to write and enjoy her time with her husband John of 42 years. If you are around Topsail Island, don't be surprised to see her and her husband out kayaking, biking or just sitting on the beach. If you're around the Appalachian Trail in Pa. around Blue Mountain you may catch them cross-country skiing, or riding the Rails of Trails on their bikes. A mother of six, grandmother of 14 (so far).

Diane spends her time writing in her journals and looking back on the answered prayers and miracles God's performed in her family's life. Working on her books, hoping that they will help and inspire others. Look for her CD's and future books. She has also written stories for children with Christian values, using her own life and children and grandchildren as characters in the stories which should be out by the end of the year.

You can contact her for speaking events at 484-894-7851

Works Cited

Kings James Bible

Phil. 1:6, Phil. 4:13, Phil. 4:8, Eph. 6: 12-17, Mark 10:27, Romans 8:28, Romans 8:31, Romans 8:35, Romans 8:39, Psalms 22:1-2, Psalms 37:25, Mat. 18:10, Mat. 24:13, Mark 10:15, Luke 18:17

Quotes:

The movie *Lord of the Rings*

Martin Luther King

Serenity Prayer, author unknown

Analogy taken from the movie *Star Wars*, the word force which was the source of good and evil power, God's Holy Spirit is our force, our power to fight against evil

Analogy of conversation between Frodo and Gandalf, we as Christians must make the best out of what we've been given